LOVE THY NAYBOR

(A Brothaz Love)

Julius Jones Present's Julian Rashko

CONTRIBUTORS

To My Mother's "Dawn Rashko," I'm Sorry ma….

I love you more than Anything ….

To My Kid's: Ruby

Olivia

Ta Kari

Jamiah

Hazel

Bracelyn Jr.

To My Nieces: Raniya

Betty Anne

And My Nephew: Psalms

Uncle Juju loves and miss Yawl!

Free Ruger (BH) Free Booka (NHB)

Free Top Hunna Ekray (BH) Free Wood chuck (NHB)

Free Makk 5 (FTB) Free Tim Tim (FTB)

Free Perico (FTB) Free Ray Black (BH)

In Loving Memory

NHB.I. P Red Haze 1 (Joel Chandler Rashko Jr)

BPS.I. P Streetz 1 F.T.P.I.P Na Na

F.T.B.I.P P Dot BPS.I. P Johntae

BPS.I. P Bhristian NTG.I. P Swag

WSP.I. P Kevo BPS.I. P YG Quon

BPS.I. P Lil E GKB.I. P D Watt

CHAPTERS

INTRODUCTION _____ 5

MAMA PACKED UP _____ 8

THE BULLYING STARTED _____ 10

EARNING OUR RESPECT _____ 14

DAY-TO-DAY STRUGGLES TURN US INTO HUSTLER _____ 18

BACK DOWN MEMORY LANE _____ 21

PRETENDING TO BE IN A GANG _____ 23

OUR FIRST ENCOUNTER _____ 25

GETTING PUT ON _____ 28

GANG LIFE _____ 32

GOING FROM STATE TO STATE _____ 35

MY BROTHAZ DEATH _____ 37

YOU CAN TELL WHO IS FAKING _____ 40

WHAT IS MORE IMPORTANT TO YOU _____ 43

THE SET UP _____ 45

IN LOVING MEMORY OF MY BROTHER _____ 50

Introduction

Julius Jones welcomes you to" Love Thy Naybor" Vol 2 A Brothaz Love more than just individuals, image let alone myth. Julian Rashko story is nonfiction in the city kids and young kids around the world can relate to. Awareness about two fatherless kids, with no proper guidance, no role models. Looking to always being accepted everywhere Julian and his brother move to. A story how kids are not being taught within each household accepting how light and dark skin children of all color is that we are all equal.

When the proper teaching is not in place at home, then it spills into the schools the streets. No one household is perfect by any means. For that reason, this" Love Thy Naybor" A Brothaz Love Vol 2 is being presented. By bringing awareness it saves countless kids in young teenagers growing up not to go down the same road Julian Rashko has, prior to his federal prison bid, he already beat a life sentence. Once you make a choice, decision to live a life of a genocide, it's a forever ending cycle.

He has seven kids out in the world that's left feeding for themselves. When you out day, evening and night with the homies, the set who is left tucking the kids in every night? Who is left feeding them day and night? Yes, Julian Rashko supported his kids yet where is he at now the message is not about what you did for the moment, it's about being there permanently by making better choices and decisions. By learning from people mistakes before you so you will stay in the right path of life.

Now you are holding up the set, riding for the set. You went to county jails and prisons, right? Who is protecting those seven children? Who is protecting his Mama? Who is protecting his sister? His family is out in the world defenseless, above all its his duty to protect not only his children and his sister in his mama.

You see is not just about you, when you decide to make choices and decisions in your life. It became a domino effect when your life is no longer balanced. Those that are the closest to you, especially your children get hurt the most. Just imagining having to now watch your children grow up through pictures now. Some of your children you don't even have a clue what is going on, due to the second you'd locked up or get sentence a certain mother of your child or children doesn't accept the calls for you to even speak to your child or children. Returning your mail, not even your own mama, not even being allowed to stay in contact with her own grand baby or babies.

Missing them precious moments, not being able to see your children walk across that stage of graduation. One of the most important accomplishments in your child children lives. After being so dedicated and committed to his set. from the second being put on to Neighborhood Rolling 20s Bloods.

All the sacrifice his freedom and put his life on the line, to now being set up by the federal informant that was awful one point in time of Blood. The twisted part there was another Blood that vouched for the persons that set up Julian. Its wild how once Julian gets locked up how, countless started kicking his back in like he was the informant. In that life everyone is in competition with you, when it supposed to be camaraderie respect and love for one another. In the end it's just a bunch of separation hate envy jealousy and what people can get out of you. I'll let you see for yourself; is this the life you want to live. Like so many others, you won't get that far so welcome to" Love Thy Naybor" Vol 2 (A Brothaz Love).

Mama Packed Up

I'm known as the first-generation Infrared 1 as well as second generation Red Haze 2. An honorable member from East Coast chapter of the Neighborhood Bloods, as well as honorary member of the West Side 29th St Neighborhood Rollin 20s Bloods. Born in Norfolk VA raised in Newport news, Virginia. Life started with a father in the navy, a mother who at the time was a preschool teacher assistant. Life started off smooth as far as living conditions up to about age 6- or 7, of course with the exception of occasionally troubled me and my siblings got into while exploring our environment.

My father's occupation caused for him to be out to sea for six months, come home for 14 days. An and ship right back out for another six months or years. I guess eventually my mother got tired of that cycle on the strain it put on their marriage. So, it led to a divorce. In from there, I would say life took a turn for the worse. My mother was still young and lovely so, I don't think she thought too far ahead. When she was fed up and determined to leave, that's what she did while my dad was out to sea. She packed us up along with what we could carry and left. We bounced around between hotel rooms and family members houses in Newport News and Hampton before my mom and dad re conceal and he moved us down to Alabama and he had now been stationed.

We stay in apartment complex in the area called Dolphin Island, which was right on the water. It was an ok spot but I guess my parents only miss each other's touch because not too long after we got there on a few love sessions, they were back to going at it a father went back out to sea. During his outing, we caught a giant hurricane that flooded our whole neighborhood and then some. We then migrated to Fairfield, Alabama where me and my brother play basketball in football for the only portion of our lives. We were good at sports, but it just wasn't really our thing. Our father never around, my mother went AWOL on the family. So, we didn't have nobody trying to help us up again and we migrated to Mobile, Alabama. Before the city, of course we got in our little trouble (mainly stealing) in this and that but this is when balance of our mixed nationality changed to us only embracing our black side.

Being raised by my mom in the areas we would live in from here on out. My dad is Italian, Irish, Portuguese. In my mom is Black. Unlike our sister, me ah my brother came out with really bright complexions in which could be mistaken for white. Spotlight was automatically put on us because we are the only two in our community this like skin.

The Bullying Started

Nobody is born gangster, and I for damn sure wasn't. I was emotional, sensitive, mama's boy at that time and the only person. I ever fought with was my brother sad to say. Mobile Alabama is where, I say my experience of bullying started. For some reason, we walked to school which was a couple of blocks away. Plenty others walk as we'll. Walking to an and back from school, it was always a group determined to hurt us. We got called white boys and got jumped on by numerous every time.

We did know fighting back sad to say, we took a beating an continued our walk. In these years, me and my brother figured that we only had each other. We had people that we would consider friends and shit, but every time we went to their neighborhood or house to play their peoples will end up jumping on us without them helping. So other than the walks to and from school, we just started keeping to ourselves and playing around the house. My mama has started dating a friend of hers that's been around since before, I was born. and once again come we packed up and went to live with him in Atlanta, Georgia. A neighborhood known as Park Place.

Now we in the hood. Mobile was bad but here.... Things got worse. Once again me and my brother are the brightest motherfuckers in the community, and we instantly became targets. Sad to say, when we got Atlanta.... I was going to the third grade and was already use to getting beat on. Just like strength or height, your heart builds a bit at a time. At this point in life, I'm still fearful emotional and sensitive. But, I'm also tired mad and someone used to this bullshit inside. So, the differences between Mobile and when we get 2 Atlanta and the bullying continuing. I will now say things like fuck you or bitch knowing be going to get beat up anyway.

The heart's building because at first, I was even scared to do that shaking my head. The wild thing is, me and my brother naturally knew how to fight. the fact is we were just scared back then. Every time we got jumped on and decided to throw a swing, it always landed and it was always effective and we would make them go harder on us. I think it scared them a little. Nobody ever tried to give us a one-on-one fight. The guy we moved in with who later became what we view as a "Step Dad" was from Chicago. An, I'm sure had his share of bullshit growing up, over time we started to resent him because he didn't step in at all. We felt he could have at least orchestrated some 1 on ones for us like we saw other dads doing. So, we could get a fair chance on some revenge.

Never got it until one day, but I'll get to that in a minute. So, we had that little resentment to us at the time. He gave us our first nicknames; change the style of clothes my mom will get us. We'd take his slang; he changed the music we listen to an most of all.... Inspire us to want to rap. him and his friends were trying to make it as rappers back then. And we used to listen and study all his shit. We even memorized it and started rapping it to everybody like it was ours, that got us some cool points laughs. Mind you this is me in the 3rd grade.

I feel like every generation grew up faster than the last but I swear I feel like I was never a kid. Is like, I couldn't afford to be, a guess it's what happens when you fall so young to try and think yourself out of detrimental situations because one thing, we never did no matter how scared we was, was run or hide. We took whatever came to us, and the trait alone played a major part when we got older and into the gang life, but I'll get to that later. now to empathize on that one day me and my brother finally got a fair chance for some revenge period leading up to that day, from the town we arrived in Park Place.

We've been jump 1000 times, punched on, spit on, choked up all krazy, hit with shit. But through these circumstances after a few months. Now we swinging back or getting a good punch in before everybody jumps in. We started getting comfortable with how life was going and just rolled with it. We were even starting to hang out with the same people that were beaten on us. I guess because they saw we were starting to fight back, and weren't going anywhere and we weren't scared of anything. They just decided to accept us as part of the community.

It was weird though because one day you'll see us running behind them playing, and the next you hearing some lady from the balcony like y'all get off them little red niggas (happen more often than you would think).

But you could tell we were earning respect on even starting to be liked by everybody. Especially after we won second place in the talent show at the "Rec Center" where me and my brother perform "My Way" by Usher laughs.

Earning Our Respect

But anyway, one day the main guy that always picked on us saw us at the bus stop waiting to go to school. He came over talking shit, pushing us the usual. I'm in the third-grade dude is in the 5th grade. A kid that was new to the neighborhood from Stone Mountain and was also in the 5th grade told dude to leave us alone. They get into its dude that pick on us was trying to choke the new kid was punching him in his shit. The bus pulled up and the driver got off and broke it up and got the new kid on the bus along with us. When me and my brother sat in our seat together, my brother said Yō.... you saw that?

I knew what he meant and I said yeah that nigga can't fight for real. We made a vow right then and there, when we catch dude solo, we were going to take out everything we been through on him. One of the popular cats in the hood stayed in our building, so everybody was usually in front of our shit. We get off the bus and head home, when we turned the corner, everybody looking at us or smiles except for dude who now had of black eye.

Everybody like damn, we done turn Yawl bright asses up! Why Yawl do him like that? Dude told everybody us in the boy jumped him and that's why his eye is blacked. We know we didn't do it, but everybody thinking we did make me feel good and even a little hyped.

Before we could say anything, somebody said that man want his ones started laughing out loud.

Isn't that some shit. After all the shit we've endured hearing a fair fight sounded like a meal for the malnutrition." It's Whatever" I said, because even though I'm the younger brother. I was protective over him as much as I could be, whether he liked it or not. I always felt like that had to go through me to touch my big brother. I always threw myself out there first (which also became a major trait when I got older and into gang life).

Anyway, two kids push him towards me and he pushed me, which was a good thing because I froze up for a second! But after he pushed me, I punch him in the mouth and it felt good. He touched his lip and looked at the blood so long that it made me look, still with my fist clenched. "Damn, I did that."

I remember thinking, and ready to do more damage. He let out a little growl and charged at me. Before he got in my arm's length he gets hit on the side of his face and drops.... My brother caught him clean and mean laughs.... This sent everybody in the uproar dude was known for picking on kids way smaller than him. So, I guess for some reason they felt like he deserved some get back because when he started to get up. I hit him again and nobody jumped in. Somebody said let him up so, I

did. He tried to charge my brother again I grabbed his shirt and swung him until he fell again. He got up and hit me with a rock.

The blood leaking from my head sent my brother over the edge. It turns in two of us jumping him an beating the shit out of him for like 3 minutes.

Somebody once again said "let him up" but one big dude in the hood that really took a liking to me and my brother said "Na fuck that, let them get theirs", and we did him dirty without anybody jumping in. Viewing the damage we did, and how further we were willing to go, spark something in both of us that would also play a major part when we got older and into the gang life. Some people first love was money, some was drugs, some was sex etc.... My first love was the feeling of being "respected". The older kids buying us ice cream from the truck, the older girls dancing on us and letting us touch them, getting called to come outside by a bunch of motherfuckers and mom like "Why they want You'll little yellow asses to come out there?

An us happy and running out the door instead of how we used to drag walking out. The older kids were always break it into an empty apartment in the hood and using it to smoke and mess with girls. They never let us smoke, but they did let us come into empty spots and be in the mix. An would see what they were doing with the girls. Finally, being treated fairly and with respect and the hood meant everything to us, a how we got it made us think that being violent was the only way to earn respect. (Which also play a major part when we've got into gang life).

Life went from us being picked on, to earning our respect, in now we being made into bullies because after a while, the older kids started telling us to beat on other kid for no reason. So desperate to keep my respect and earn cool points, we did what we were told, all the while the real me inside feeling bad for these kids. But we felt like if we said no or didn't do what was asked of us, they would turn on us again, sad to say. After a while, we got kind of numb to it and came all around comfortable with how life was. Finally at max comfort, thinking this what life going to be for next couple years.

Day-To-Day Struggles Turn Us into Hustler

Mind you all this transpired in one year. 1999 to the beginning of 2000. My mom and step pops decided they not going work and once again, mom pack us up and we dip headed back to Virginia. While she is weeks pregnant with my little sister. When my mom and dad divorced, I can't remember us staying in one place more than a year. Until we landed in the one neighborhood we would call "home" rather we live there or not (I'll get back to that). We came back to Virginia in for some time as we usually did when my mom was figuring out her next move, we stayed in hotels and with family members.

We finally got stable when my mom found an apartment, a blessing because now me, my brother and older sister or what you consider "Bad Kids" at this point and the shit we doing is causing problems between my mom and the family members we end up staying with. But of course, at the time we don't care and don't understand the pressure and stress we put us more moms. We get into that apartment right on time for her to have my baby sister in good space. Up until the 3rd grade, I did the typical okay for kids and shit, but after leaving Atlanta, and how life looked at me now.

I went into 4th grade worried about everything but education. I just wanted to be class clown, mess with girls talk shit and go home to play outside. We never hung around nobody our age which is another reason I said I never felt like a kid.

We running behind grown men viewing what they were into an when they would say" take yell bad asses to the park or something" we will be like "Na...." and stay with them an end up getting a piece of what we consider" wisdom" after seeing them making a sale or doing a drug an asking "What's that?" How much you sell it for? For whatever reason this is the knowledge we wanted to obtain instead of some Social Studies or English. After getting my mom kicked out of that apartment in 100 others, we ended staying with a relative who stayed in uptown Newport News out of hood called Warwick Town Houses.

Warwick Town Houses one of three projects also Jennifer Square and Colina Rood Square) based on 2 streets (Sharon Dr. A Savage Dr.) that runs through all three hoods basically making it one big neighborhood with a lot to do. This will be the place we consider ourselves jumping off the porch it is here where we would first dabble in hustling, robbing, B&E's of course more fighting shooting and eventually.... gang banging. As far as the money aspect the first thing we started doing was breaking an end entry. It all started from a mom's telling us she not getting us a PlayStation because we aren't doing shit in school.

The next night, I'm in the room watching TV my brother come in with a PlayStation." Where the fuck you get that? In them shoes? Let me get them? "I said, hell na, you going to come with me and get your own" he told me. That night we broke in like 6 spots. I say come we were so mad that moms wouldn't get us shit and so happy to find out how we could get what we want that we got addicted to doing B&E's. Moms use to see the shit we were bringing in and barked but knew she couldn't really do nothing. We were gone. We got so good at it that our hustle became to Katz that was getting money in our neighborhood will put orders in for shit usual (electronics, game systems, computers, etc.) We would go get it and they will pay us.

We gave them great prices and they always brought what we came with. We didn't even really care what we made, long as it was consistent, we just wanted some money, shoe clothes, games and guns. The first beef we inherited was with the kids our age and a little older that was in a hood just fence over from our hood known as Aqueduct. The main projects people think of when referring to uptown, has the most reputation for bullshit.

Back Down Memory Lane

Started off the same as the rest, them thinking light skin is a form of weakness or some shit. They'd come through, press one of their homies to fight one of us soon as they homie get hit too hard, they all jump in that went on for a while around this time people were getting murdered and shot and all that but it was still a lot of fighting going on than compared to nowadays. Back then people still in the hood wanted to be known us" nice with the hands" slap boxing and fighting was the thing but after a while shit got worse and guns became a big part of life, I get to that in a second.

Gang banging.... a sentimental topic to me. It's all I care to live and breathe since, I was 12- 13 years old. Is the first thing that ever took the most serious in my life. It's what I put overall things until, I was finally brought to my senses that there is love bigger than the gang after all those years I'll get to that, but how it all started.... We first saw signs a reputation being done in Alabama by the GD's they were throughout our area in Mobile and even the kids our age was repping because of their older brothers or family members is just what we saw nothing in, US ever even thought at the time to involve in any of that stuff we had enough problems because of our complex laughs....

What's crazy is, my first time trying to kill a Crip was in the 3rd grade while we were in Atlanta, the memory just hit me. Where we live, they weren't really gang banging yet they had the little neighborhood gangs in groups but it was this one Crip from Louisiana that was grown and out of school that would have kids out there saying "Wess Cracking "Cuz and throwing up C's. One day me and my brother walking from the park, and for whatever reason out of nowhere he hangs us in this tree by our underwear, laughs.... We were up there turning in circles until my sister saw us in got somebody to get us down. I felt like Doughboy in "Boys N Da Hood" when he tried to get his brother ball back.

"I want to kill that motherfucker" I thought. Two days later. I see him and got scared and ran back in the house. I was scared but I was also mad. I remember my step dad had a gun in his room closet I ran and got it and ran outside I walked up to him and pulled it from behind my back, he said do it, I dare you little nigga. I was scared as shit, my hand shaking retarded but I was tired of everything. I close my eyes and pulled the trigger "past" is the sound it made. Yō, the shit was a BB gun Yō.... Damn. Dude took it, smack the shit out of me and dropped me off course and said" thought that would hurt me little nigga?" or something like that.

And pick me up. The dude said" I like that, got to get you a real one 'Cuz and gave me the shit back. I ran back in the house and put the gun back laughs out loud... That's one of my most memorable moments. I didn't know there were fake guns and real guns at the time. I just wanted to kill him. For putting this on display like that for the neighborhood to see and laugh at us.

Pretending To Be in A Gang

But anyway, our first real knowledge of gang banging came from movies of course. We were kids running around talking about "Deuce Here"! After seeing movies like South Central, an after viewing" Colors" "Blood in Blood out'" that movie went Denzel Washington played the school principal in the in the Crip and Brims would get into it "Hard Lessons". We would play fight in argue over who was going to be the Brim or the Crip we both wanted to be Brims it made me and my brother go from the mind frame that we only needed each other to we need some homies.

One thing we never did in public anyway was act like Bloods or Crips. We knew not to fake it. What we did do is start our own gang with some friends in 6th grade. At passage middle school called "Ghetto Ghost's" my brother had failed the 4th grade. So, we ended up in the 6th grade together. Him on one hallway me on the other end. He had his friends, I had mine and we put them all on and brought everything together. We would tag the school and have slap boxing and fight in bathroom we had even got to a point where an older gang in the school known as "Drop Set" a gang started in the courthouse green neighborhood of uptown.

Who later became an enemy to us as Bloods because they affiliation with the Crips we grew up beefing with. Had giving us respect and claimed allies with us. We eventually got targeted by the principle in security for the bull shit we was doing and was being looked for but they didn't know who was who.

But thanks to this one person who got caught with a paper that had all our names an alias on it along with the gang at the top, we all started getting called to the office 1 by 1 into this room that had a round table in it. Some of us sat down some stood around us like a Mafia movie. A police officer, the security guards and the principal told us if any of us seen with each other after the meeting we will be expelled and others bullshit. So, shit died down in school and only few of us saw each other outside of school so the gang eventually died out.

Our First Encounter

That was our first taste of repping anything in gang life. After that, that summer my mom sent me and my brother to the store to get some shit. When we get to the store it's a Hispanic dude standing in front of it just posted. "Sup wit yawl? he says," Sup with you? We speak. He asked if we were banging my brother said no but we want to. I noticed the gold flag in his back left pocket and asks" What you are? he said 'Almighty Latin King." We never heard of it at that time so, we thought it was his own gang. We stood there talking for minute and asking questions until he finally said "Yawl want to be Latin Kings" I'm like but we aren't Latin.

He asks was our nationality, we told him black and he said black people could be Latin Kings. We said alright Kool," What we got to do? He said it takes time to become official so we had to just move with him. We agree in started being around him every day for about a week or so trying to become official, but before we get their bullshit transpires. Come to find out, my cousin from known area known as the "Warwick Lawns" section of Uptown had gotten this dude out they hood. When he went out there on the same shit. We had started bring him around our hood and neighborhood (Warwick Town Houses).

Warwick Lanes and Aqueduct all one accord known as "Da Lanes 2 Da Dust" strip. So, one thing goes on in one hood, all three going to know somebody told my cousin the Latin king nigga was now fucking around our hood and trying to recruit us. We came home from somewhere that data everybody telling us he came through looking for us, and my cousin in his niggas saw him and they fucked him up bad. We never saw him again after that, which left a bad impression with us so we felt like it's not what we were meant to be. That same year 2004, I can't recall what he did but my mom kicked my brother out and he disappeared for a few days.

When he came back to the hood, he had a red bandana out his back right pocket and a swollen eye. From the beginning, when we first really started indulging in the streets and new, we were going to gang bang we wanted to be Bloods we had numerous people trying to recruit us but we would decline because those individuals weren't the type we wanted to fuck with every day and be obligated to. We knew when we became official with whatever gang we got with, and the homies that would accept us, that we would devote our life to it an them. Coming up the way we did, anybody that would say or show us "I got your back, "You need anything," If you going, I'm going," "let's go half," "I got it, "We doing it together," etc....

Any type shit like that, you had every bit of me and my brothers love, loyalty and respect and without hesitation we would put our life on the line for you, which of course.... us not being able to see thoughts, intentions and motives of the fake and non-genuine became our downfall and numerous occasions and lessons we will learn through trial and error that most people are underserving of your authenticity.

Getting Put On

So, as careful as we were being, when I saw the red flag in his pocket.

You must have run across a reputable homey he felt was our caliber" Sup with that? What we doing? I asked my big brother," come here.... he told me, and started walking to the side of the building where most of the fights in our hood took place. He showed me the handshake and as soon as we locked the "B", he punched me in my shit. I always was the harder hitter, but my brother is faster with agility in his hard as well. We fought hard until he said we were done. He gave me the bandana he had gotten from who put on.

I used it to wipe the blood from my mouth "gotten meet some people "he told me. That night we walked to another hood and I met the person who put my brother on. I took a second beating from the homies that night before being given the shake and hug in props on how I got down. Safe to say, at 13 years old it felt like I was reborn and my only priority in life was to be the best blood I can be. My everyday mission was to become feared, respected, love, connected on in the early 2000's.... A Crip Killer. Our rivals growing up was the 10-1 Mafia Crips in anybody cool with them.

After being put on the set, we dived head first into the beef with them not knowing or caring how to be started or we were told was on site with all Crips on upheld that for years. Affiliations killed friendships, limited social networking, put distance between family members and more. In the year 2021, in which I am writing this I have been a non-stop active member for 18 years day in and day out. I have been shot numerous times on different occasions, stabbed, in a thousand fights jumped a million times, shot at 100, incarcerated under force pretenses from police wanting me that bad and people willing 2 throw my name in situations. I've never been in just to help themselves, told on by people I considered homies, family and friends just to help themselves after being the most loyal to everyone.

I've had police beat on me and tried to defecate my character for not cooperating or giving them anything they wanted. I've lost numerous people. I love to prison system and death, the most notable and tragic in my life that actually caused a change in my thoughts, feelings and emotions in a way. I can't explain was the loss of my Big Brother" Red Haze 1" one to the hands of a Crip. While we were in New York for my birthday which was also all Mother's Day that year 2014. To isolate my brother's story in a summary very quickly. First off, we learned everything through trial and error. There was common sense gifted to us as well as morals a principal. I looked up to my Big Brother because he' did" everything.

I "felt" and help bring it "out" of me and "spoke" on everything that didn't need to be "said" but had to be "heard". So, I would know that, I was "doing right" (Hopefully it makes sense to you). Our reputation means everything to us and we will rather be killed than be viewed as disloyal, dishonorable, in a snitch, untrustworthy a coward etc.... That's just what it is and that's what was installed in me from him. One day we got jumped by some Crips dudes from Aqueduct some downtown dudes that were with them. We shot one on ones with two Crips first because two dudes that moved to our hood from New Orleans after Katrina hit that were boxers. And on some gangster shit for real. One of them was also a Crip we didn't find out until we already had mad love for each other. So, it didn't matter. Said they not letting them jump us.

The group said they not trying to jump (bullshit) they Crip's homies just want to get down with us. I went first and beat old boy up; my brother went next and punched another dude a couple of times before the group said that's enough and acted like they were leaving. Slim an V (the brother from N.O) dapped us up with props and respect before getting in the car and leaving out the hood. The group saw both of them leave and started walking back towards us. We have got the two girls we were with to hold our bandanas, we got them back and put them back on our heads and saw group coming. They walked up like they were giving us props but when they got close enough to do swing at us, (we saw a coming). We ducked, they missed, then everybody jumped on us. The usual. They did them, we got some links in the police slid through and we all scattered.

That night, our homie heard what happened and came through our hood and brought us a gun. We were glad because we knew after the way, we did the two Crip dudes, they were coming back. Mane they came back the next day. My brother grabbed the gun and we ran outside. Soon as we got to the end of our building where they were at, my brother lifted the gun to shoot. Before he squeezed the trigger, police turn in our hood. They saw him aiming, he tossed it behind a bush as they pulled up (not knowing if they saw him with it or not). They pulled in our lot made both of us get down, the other went to the bush and get the gun.

They grabbed my brother a left as, I laid there hoping they were going take me too, but they didn't. My brother did almost three years in Juvenile Prison. While, I took on all our beef, by myself, which made more different by time he got out. A gun became my best friend over those years, he was gone. An, I started making a big name in a rep for myself. As a little homie or Yg (Young Gangster) (in which I took pride in being).

Gang Life

I gradually but quickly became categorized in the top five most reputable Bloods in my region and known for busting my gun fighting anybody. Zero tolerance for Crips, Robbing, and taking over an area known as Beechmont and making it a Bloods 'Safe Haven" or "Turf". My brother will hear about everything I was into and had gone. In as sad as it may sound to those who haven't indulged or condoned in the gang banging lifestyle.... he was proud of me. He was doing same thing I was doing just behind the wall. Advancing in the lifestyle, earning respect putting in work, loyalty to the set, riding for cause (that being whatever the cause called for).

To show how true we are to this and all in for it. For whatever reason we over flood with passion for this shit. So, we never looked at anything we did in the name of "Blood" as wrong. It felt like we were "supposed" to be doing and nobody could tell us different. When my big brother was nearing the end of his sentence and waiting to go halfway house. I was 15 in had gotten arrested while walking my older sister to the corner store in my hood. I was charged with armed robbery, tried as an adult in moved from Juvenile Detention to the city jail with the grown-ups. It was a drastic change but I adapted quickly had to.

My most moment from that experience was how crowded the jail was. Two major sweeps had just taken place in which a gang from 17th street known as' Dump Squad" and a rival gang from round 36st known as "Wick Mafia" had caught indictments an had the jail packed with four people in two-man cells. It was that, and getting jumped on block "6G" by 10-1 Mafias and Hoovers being that, I was the only Blood on the unit. I eventually got helped by one of the Wick Mafia niggas, who eventually turned Blood. I ended up beating the robbery after the "alleged" victim said he was promised help with the charge he caught if he helped him get me off to the street. He claimed they didn't help him and he felt bad because he didn't know how young, I was.

In the mist of this, I was robbed of the experience of viewing the birth of my first-born daughter "Ruby" who was born only months after I turned 16. I was acquitted night before my brother was expected to leave from the halfway house. When I came home of course one of the first things I did was spend some time with my daughter. But that wasn't my only focus. Not only me but a few of my homies had got into situations with the law and a couple of us were gone. Which the Crips took as an opportunity to invade Beechmont. In try to claim it as theirs that had more of my force than playing "daddy," sad to say.

I jumped out their head first with my remaining homies and did what we needed to reclaim our hood. Unlike my brother, I had plenty of time to develop a lot of street smarts over those years he was gone. I had gotten good at robbing, carrying and using guns, leadership in other bullshit. I can't file taxes on, but at the time.... It was everything. After hearing about everything, I was on while he was locked, he came home feeling the need to go harder than me. I guess it was a Big Brother "pride" thing. He wasn't taking my advice, heeding's my warnings, hearing my opinions nothing He. jump out there shooting and robbing everything and within exactly 30 days of his release he was back in jail charged with armed robbery in which he beat but received five years day for day for the fire arm he had on him when he got picked up.

Going From State to State

While he was doing his bid, I was still in the streets gang banging, robbing, traveling doing the same shit in different states. Building a more reputation and respect levels from other sets in different gang's spreading my name nationwide (how we supposed to do). I started to go frequent places like New York, California, Georgia, North Carolina etc... So, when my brother came home, I wanted him to see some new scenery, have some new experience. Because at one point before his bid our hood (Sharon and Savage Dr) was our world. Gradually, we started playing the whole Uptown. After we both were kicked out of public schools in started on going to Alternative Schools, (I went to PMI which is no longer around. My brother went to Enterprise, got kicked out and went to Jackson Academy).

Where between those schools that was mixed with kids from throughout the whole city and us occasionally ending up in the Juvenile Detention Center for bullshit. We got cool with people from downtown. In started playing the whole city as well as Hampton, an eventually the whole" 7 cities" region on the gang banging strength. But that's as far as my brother got before doing those stents behind the wall. So, when he came home, I wanted to share my reach with him and introduce him to some good people. I've met over the years. Even though, I talked about my brother everywhere I went so people would know him before they met him. I wanted him to build his own national report the way I did.

Before he even got out that year, I had my mind on spending my birthday in New York with the homies. I've grown to love up there, along with some day ones of mine from V.A. I was in Charlotte NC for the birth of my youngest son not too long after my brother came home. I had left my brother with a couple of 100 and a half pound of weed along with some clothes to get him going. (The best I could do at the time). Not too long after his release he had got into a situation with one of the homies.

In a Latin king we were cool with causing a war and him to skip out on his probation meetings giving him a violation as well, I didn't find out until around in" Da News" to scoop him and my homies to head-to-head to N.Y. They had a spot out Aqueduct or "Da Duck" (after years of tension we began frequenting out there just because) and when I pull into the neighborhood it was police everywhere. I pulled up to the spot, they be in view two of my day ones in front of the spot. I asked him where my brother was at, they said the police was just chasing him and he got away (that's my dawg) blood was exclusive as a mother fucker. After sitting around for a little bit. I get call from my brother saying he was over the fence in our hood ducked off in one of our people spot in Warwick Town Houses.

My Brothaz Death

Instantly we hop in the whip, went through a scooped him up before hopping straight on the road to New York. We made it to Brooklyn and homies started pulling up from everywhere. They always show mad love when I touched the city. Everybody embrace my brother with love and respect an, I could view him loving being somewhere else as we walked through Brooklyn. Him taking in the scenery comfortably. This is one of the main cities, I know most about a how to move as far as New York. So, other than the gun he had on him, he felt safe with his little brother. Plans were made before we got there, but a pawn arrival shit change on we had to improvise.

We ended up in Jamaica Queens (a city I didn't frequent over my years of going to NY) in which it was suggested that the park up the street from where we were, was a good spot to grill and kick it with the homies for the B-Day. Me and a few homies slid to Ray Wilkins Park as our ride went back to Brooklyn to grab my brother and a few more homies after a minute of kicking it and watching homies fucking around on the basketball court. Something we didn't realize until we thought back on it is somehow, we became the only people in the park. At first every court was filled, kids running around everywhere, tents on the other side where people were doing shit.

Out of nowhere, right under our noses, like everybody was given a warning or alert to vacate. Everybody but us. Talking to one of my day one N.Y homies somebody said "Red" they go "Haze". I looked back and saw him walking up and we locked eyes throwing up the set to each other, I went back to talking with my N.Y homies until my brother reached us and my last time hearing him speak was "Wess Rollin Bloods?" Before I turn in dapped him up. When we lock the set, out of nowhere.... "What Cracking.... (Boom! Boom!)" In broad daylight. All in all, a brother was struck in the head by one of the first bullets.

Caught in the moment I don't remember our hands detachment. As well as viewing him hit the ground. Everybody scattered out of the park and when I didn't view my brother in neither of the two groups, we were now separated into, I ran back in the park to where we were at the find my big brother laying in the same place he had been standing. Viewing him panting and moving the way he was, I figure he was going to be okay if we just got him to a hospital. In the midst of me over him talking to him and trying to get him to open his eyes. My day one homie from VA started grabbing me up and pulling me by my shirt "Damu! Damu come on!" he said before once again.... Boom! Boom! Boom! Bullets start whizzing pass my ear, one even grazing my leg as my homie continue pulling me out of the way.

In the end my brother was transported to Jamaica Hospital where after my mother and others back home were notified of the situation, made their way to Queens. My brother was later pronounced "brain dead" in which they said was no need to continue life support. Mother's Day 2014 as well as my birthday was taking off life support and watched him take his last breath. With him went a piece of my man, on siblings, our day ones and loved ones.... but it took a different toll on me and I can't explain. I've lost homies and family; I've seen people die and get killed. But there's just things you feel like can't happen to you, or the ones you closest to, so when it does.... it changes you, really just changes you.

My brother was the biggest lost, I think I'll ever feel other than to lose my mother or my kids.

You Can Tell Who Is Faking

I can't say nobody really guided me for real, I can only emphasize those that show me something worth value. Other than my step dad "Sketch" I referred to in my story, I would say a non-affiliated OG of me and my brother that we came up under and Warwick Town Houses name "Sean Don" who's doing life and State Prison. Just watching how he move gave us mental notes at a young age how to be "stand up niggas" as well as his uncle" Big Guns" who I would consider a non-affiliated double Og (also from my hood) to me. When I was tried as an adult and sent to the City Jail, after the incident "6G" with the Crips. I ended up on "5B" with him in which he looked out for me and showed me the ropes.

Another person would be my older cousin Antonio "Tone" Fuller who also doing a life sentence. Just another "stand up nigga" type that you can honestly say" they don't make them like that no more." That me in my brother value having respect from. You got those people you don't have to question; you know they're going be solid no matter what and that's what he rubbed off on me. Another one is B Mook AKA Mob 1 also known as Red Haze 3. This who put me and my brother on the "Damu Life" and saw something in us that made him want put us under his wing. In his life on the line for us. He became a 3rd brother, an after passing of my real one, him being one of two people. I can still get that real brother field from along with Reese aka "K Rock".

These two are who, I would consider my day one's. Those two, me and my brothers along with our young homie Tee black came up in this together from the start and will till the finish (love Yawl niggas, on NH). When Blood became a fad in 2005 from little Wayne, Dip set other rappers, there was hundred Bloods uptown by 2006.... There was like 10 of us (real ones). Niggas doing 30 days in Juvenile, come home and stop repping. Get in one fight be like this isn't for me. Get jump one time this isn't for me. Get shot at (not even hit) this life isn't for me. Call out by a homie to see where the hands at, this isn't for me.

Motherfucker's love doing handshakes, throwing up signs, wearing bandanas and yelling Soo Whoop. When shit laid back to look cool but when it was time to lookout for a homie or put some work in to earn your keep, we always ended beating somebody up and kicking them out the hood.... Every time! And it will be the same old homies putting the work in. Of course, we were told that it was something that could rush your death date, and no good to be a part of. But when you actually are in the streets everybody knows that you would be a part of some group. Rather you and your neighborhood friends make one, you and your hustling homies give yourself a little title.

You in some friends make a rap group with a name that, you're are standing behind.... I knew I wanted to be a part of something greater something bigger than my city my state. In all actuality gang nation are creating more bonds and relationships from unlimited distance than anything else, in the love be real. I can go anywhere and ran into another Blood as genuine as me. Though it's more fake ones than real ones. When you run into another real one, you know he got you like you got him 'til you'll depart. To be able to tell the difference comes with experience but even then, the faker's the infiltrators get better at what they do to fool us into thinking we around good homies for whatever motive or intent they have.

What Is More Important to You

Anyway, you got to have a team in the streets or allies or family. I'm say a real frontline homie that involves in all activities for the set will not have to question the love, loyalty, a respect he getting is real. Me personally, I value being a soldier in the process of earning respect because you have "receipts" and "vouchers" from the set and the homies no, they can trust you. I never tried to skip steps and get into a position of power. I didn't "deserve" unlike all these overnight Ogs nowadays. You can tell who really been living the life doing everything they should. Because they are respected as Ogs before they even became one.

I wanted people to respect my "name" not my status. It's a million gang members out here insecure about their status, love, respect and loyalty from their homes because they know they never did shit to "deserve" it. I have a few different views on that. First and foremost, if you waited until you got famous to want to affiliate yourself with a gang it's only for either protection or clout or both and will not get you respected as a member it will get you "used". Mother fuckers got people thinking "Rich is gangster' which is unlikely. True indeed if you rich, you can do what you want....

Just as long as you don't do it where niggas really doing that understand? Just like if you waited until you became in adult to gang bang or affiliate with something, the same phrase will apply. You weren't been doing, why start now? These are the people that are insecure about who they are and do dumb shit and spend unnecessary time trying to prove themselves (too no naval) and reality hit them so hard they found dead somewhere. Tryna be something they not, do something they don't, go somewhere they can't.

Force on living a good life and doing good for some people, get more respect for that than what you "trying" to do. It kills me that people want so much street cred, gangster, reputation in respect for shit they never did. Niggas don't realize you get more respect for being yourself. On the other hand, if you were involved in all activities and made it through these obstacle course before catching a break and getting on.... Proud of you Blood on NH.... I have seven kids' homie and of course not. Simply, I'm of loving caring father that "Really Cares" about my kid's well-being and their outcome. Over the years although, I still put on for the set, more of my force became being father. From the love, I received from my kids, to the respect. I felt from their mothers. It seems as though I was doing great until my incarceration.

The Set Up

Touchy subject right here and I want to make sure, I cover all of bases of how, I feel at this point in my life. First and foremost, I love Damu. I love the members (the real ones) I love being a part of its on, I've never regretted it joining. and I never thought of denouncing myself as a member. I can't even explain to anybody while my passion runs so deep for something that has been the cause of the most bullshit in my life. In yet, I still love it as much as I did from when I first got put on. This life has caused some of the best memories. I can recall as well as the worst situations.

I've ever been in that, I wouldn't have if, I would've chosen another route. I would never blame "Blood" though, I did this to myself. Aside of this life that, I have I have some kind of resentment for. Is the fact that yes you meet good homies that love the life just as much as you but it's also an icebreaker for faker an infiltrator that you would never even give a head nod to as you walk past them. Leeway to engage in the conversation or politics with you to simply off the strength that they are member, and you being a genuine. Damu, you feel obligate to acknowledge that fact and give them your time not knowing them from nothing in if they had ill motives or intent.

If they do just from that icebreaker off the strength of "Blood" .... You now on his line. Unlike the infiltrators, you can sense a good homie when you around 1 and knowing that usually gets use against us. Knowing we not going to snitch, we willing to put in work, we would give who got love for our last. In which you giving the infiltrator "the benefit of doubt" until they show otherwise." Some leverage in life because they got someone credible to help them rather it's telling on you to get out of a situation or keep using you to get into a better situation. Anyway, I showed a homie I had love for and known for years away to get some good money besides drugs because like myself.

He wasn't really good at being a hustler I mean; I knew how to sell drugs but, in my position, a how my heart is. I was always looking out for homies in not getting up how, I was supposed to be. Shit was going faster than it was coming because I'm always adding another responsibility or a priority to myself without realizing it. So, even though, I was not broke and new how to get money. I was setting myself up to fail. The way my city is and how we grew up in it, our first priority was to always have a gun. It doesn't matter if we broke with nowhere to go and nothing else to show real bad news VA niggas always got a gun or guns. Through all my days of trial and error with drug dealing when I looked around and realized. I effortlessly kept numerous guns in my possession, they soon became my profession.

From bargaining prices to the lowest possible and reselling in my region for 50 to $100 extra. It grew to going other places where a gun, I'm getting for 150 to $200 is getting sold full 5-6 or $700.00. In this, I found my lane and stayed in it flawlessly for years until the homie. I was saying I had love for that. I had put on with the same hustle introduced me to another homie that he vouched up and down for. As a good homie (but didn't know from shit) and said we should do business with him because he local and willing to pay dog top dollar for guns he was going out of the region himself. Meaning, I didn't have to go out the region anymore for the money.

I was looking for but regardless of that. I only agreed off the strength of the homie vouching for this nigga thinking he really knew this man (which he didn't at all). Eventually, I got real cool with the nigga. Embrace him as homie and fucking with him on the regular for years and out of nowhere he disappears. That's in 2016, I effortlessly move low key making it hard for anyone to look in on my routine or whereabouts. But in 2019, I was in an altercation in which, I was shot in hospitalized. The feds kept tabs on me in as soon as, I was able to walk again.

I was picked up for a gun and drug trafficking. Over the years, I've seen people I'm familiar with getting picked up by the feds but I had no business dealing with them. So, I didn't think I had anything to worry about. Still on the land at the time after "Monster" (which is the name the person I was introduced to me too by my so-called homie was going by) had disappeared. I didn't notice that all those people started getting picked up soon as he vanished at the time. I'm still trying to get in touch with him a sell him guns. One day I just say fuck it and stopped it looking for him.

I get wind not too long later that it was said "Monster" was getting everybody locked up. I saw no black and white or anything figure me and him had bone a genuine bond on that' he wouldn't do me like that even if he was" .... I thought wrong. After getting locked, my second or third meeting with my lawyer he brings a bunch of CDs. What are those? I ask, "Just look" he said and starts playing them on his computer. Mann.... it was recordings of every time I've been around "Monster." He had a camera in his glasses, buttons on his shirt. A bubblehead on his dashboard, using a Bluetooth wireless headset to record audio in all.

He was like J Reed off" Into Deep" with LL Cool J On the videos. He was meeting with meeting with the feds getting wired up and speaking on some "yes sir, no sir' shit, then meeting up with me on some what's up Blood, love you Blood "shit." On one of the recordings, I had just had my twins and one of them kept almost dying and I couldn't control my emotions or stop the tears. He was recording me the whole time and acting like he cared fake consoling me portraying to be a friend. Sad Mane.... Sad Yō.

Anyway, not long after, I view those CDs with all the "Controlled Buys". I was given a copy of my motion of discovery and found out not only did monster set me up, but the person who introduced us also told on me as well as others with statements dating back to the early 2000s. I thought I had trust issues before, it is now multiplied by infinity. This being my first real big I figure I get around 60 to 70 months but thanks to enhancements from people statements, in one of list my charges carrying a mandatory minimum.

I was given 106 months in the federal prison system. I'm forever Neighborhood Blood. I love my family and I love my real ones but my force will be different upon release. Rather not even put myself in a situation that will take me away from my kids or my fam again. We need more official people on the land helping push especially the youth in better directions instead of always being the scapegoats for the frauds. That can care less about who they fuck over in the process of trying to live their best life. Those who've considered joining the life, do something different…. life is meant to "enjoy".

Love Thy Naybor

….

Infrared 1

In Loving Memory of my brother

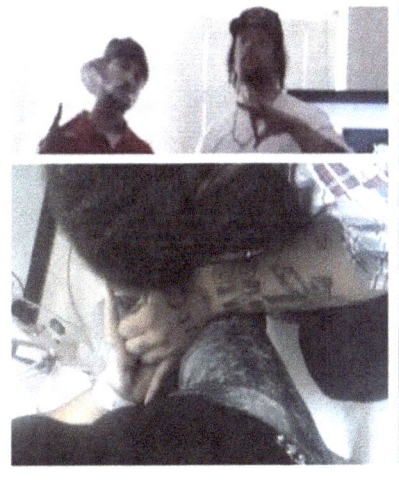

www.ingramcontent.com/pod-product-compliance
Lightning Source LLC
LaVergne TN
LVHW020416070526
838199LV00054B/3631